SMART TECHNOLOGY

Megan Blakemore and Alexis Roumanis

www.av2books.com

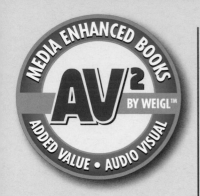

AV² provides enriched content that supplements and complements this book. Weigl's AV² books strive to create inspired learning and engage young minds in a total learning experience.

Your AV² Media Enhanced books come alive with...

Audio
Listen to sections of the book read aloud.

Key Words
Study vocabulary, and complete a matching word activity.

Video
Watch informative video clips.

Quizzes
Test your knowledge.

Embedded Weblinks
Gain additional information for research.

Slide Show
View images and captions, and prepare a presentation.

Try This!
Complete activities and hands-on experiments.

... and much, much more!

Go to **www.av2books.com**, and enter this book's unique code.

BOOK CODE

AVU 5 4 8 6 6

AV² by Weigl brings you media enhanced books that support active learning.

Published by AV² by Weigl
350 5th Avenue, 59th Floor
New York, NY 10118
Website: www.av2books.com

Library of Congress Control Number: 2017962147

ISBN 978-1-4896-7582-8 (hardcover)
ISBN 978-1-4896-7915-4 (softcover)
ISBN 978-1-4896-7583-5 (multi-user eBook)

Printed in the United States of America in Brainerd, Minnesota
1 2 3 4 5 6 7 8 9 0 22 21 20 19 18

042018
120817

Project Coordinator: Jared Siemens   Designer: Ana María Vidal

Every reasonable effort has been made to trace ownership and to obtain permission to reprint copyright material. The publishers would be pleased to have any errors or omissions brought to their attention so that they may be corrected in subsequent printings.

Weigl acknowledges Getty Images, Shutterstock, Newscom, iStock, and Alamy as its primary image suppliers for this title.

First Published by North Star Editions in 2017

Content Consultant: Bruce McMillin, Professor of Computer Science, Missouri University of Science and Technology

Contents

Self-balancing scooters, or Segways, are smart toys. The wheels are connected to a sensor pad that keeps the board balanced.

Smart Toys

Your hands grip the steering wheel. You race down the street and round a tight curve. As you pull on the brake, the go-kart drifts sideways. It's like a race car in a movie! The go-kart comes to a stop. You take off your helmet and get out of the driver's seat. This isn't any old go-kart. It's a smart go-kart.

What makes it smart? An adult can control how fast it goes. The adult can also make sure the go-kart stays within a certain area. You cannot travel too far or get lost. An adult can even stop the go-kart with a button. This can help prevent a crash.

Kids can drive smart go-karts at amusement parks, such as Legoland. Employees can control the speed of a vehicle with the use of a remote.

A smart go-kart is only one example of a smart toy. Many other toys can be programmed using an **app** on your phone or tablet. But smart technology isn't just for toys. There are **smartphones**, smart houses, and even smart cities.

Some smart toys can be assembled by hand and controlled with a computer.

A smart toy called **BB-8** is controlled with the use of an app. It can travel a distance of about **100 feet** (30 meters) from its user.

The PowerUp Dart is an app-controlled **paper airplane**. It can travel at speeds up to **15 miles** (25 kilometers) per hour.

Chapter 2

Amazon's Alexa is a smart assistant accessed through its Echo Dot device that can place online orders, search the internet, take notes, provide a weather forecast, and play music.

The Internet of Things

Smart technology refers to everyday devices that can be connected to the internet. Connecting to the internet can make a device more **interactive**. A device using smart technology also has the ability to learn. It picks up on its user's patterns or habits and makes changes accordingly. For example, a smart TV could learn a person's favorite shows and offer new episodes as soon as the TV is turned on.

Some people use the term *Internet of Things* when talking about smart technology. When an object is connected to the internet, the object can receive information. For instance, a smart doorbell may use a camera to recognize people's faces. The doorbell tells its owners whether a friend or a stranger is at the door.

Fitness Trackers

Many people use fitness trackers. These people want to know what happens to their bodies when they exercise. A program gathers **data** for heart rate, respiration, body temperature, and air temperature. The fitness tracker then gives feedback to the wearer. A tracker might tell the wearer to drink more water or to get moving.

Another example is a smart alarm clock. An alarm clock might get an update that Saturday's soccer practice was canceled. Then the alarm clock will not go off, allowing the user to get some extra sleep.

Rami is a smart alarm clock made for kids. It can track sleep patterns, play music, and glow when it is time to wake-up.

Giving Instructions

Whenever a person operates a device, he or she is giving the device instructions. For example, when someone flips a light switch, he is giving the light instructions to turn on. Smart technology sends those instructions in a new way. It sends the instructions over the internet.

The smart object, such as a smart light, is connected to the internet. An app is also connected to the internet. The app might be on a smartphone or tablet. This allows the user to connect with the smart object. Wireless **networks** mean devices do not have to be in the same city.

Users can control devices in their homes with the use of a smart home app. With apps such as SmartThings and WeMo, users can connect their coffeemakers, lights, and garage doors to their smartphones.

Some smart refrigerators know what food items are in the fridge. They are able to let users know what they will need to add to their shopping list.

Smart Houses

Smart home devices can control security, entertainment systems, and more. Instead of using her keys, a homeowner can use a smart lock. The smart lock senses that her phone is near and automatically unlocks the door for her. The owner can also speak to her TV and ask it to play her favorite show. Smart trash cans keep track of what she throws away and can order replacements.

Smart technology has the ability to learn. For example, a smart **thermostat** uses sensors to keep track of when the user is home. Over time, the thermostat learns the user's patterns and adjusts the temperature automatically. The user can also use an app to set his or her home's temperature from anywhere. So, if he or she forgets to turn off the air conditioner when leaving the house, it can be done on the go.

The average American household can save about 23 percent on their heating and cooling costs with a smart thermostat.

A smart house can also give helpful feedback. For instance, a smart toilet can give its users health feedback. It analyzes the volume and makeup of a person's waste. This information could alert the person to health problems before he or she even feels sick.

A Famous Smart House

Bill Gates, the founder of Microsoft, may have the world's most famous smart house. If you visited him, you would receive an electronic chip that you could program with temperature and music preferences. The lights would turn on before you entered a room. The house would know your favorite music and play it for you. And if you and your friend preferred different types of music, the house would try to find something in between.

For elderly people, the house can remind them to take their medications. It can also call the doctor if they are sick. This lets older people live in their own houses for as long as possible.

Senior citizens can program their smart home to call a paramedic if they cannot reach a phone. A smart home can also be set to monitor the vital signs of its residents.

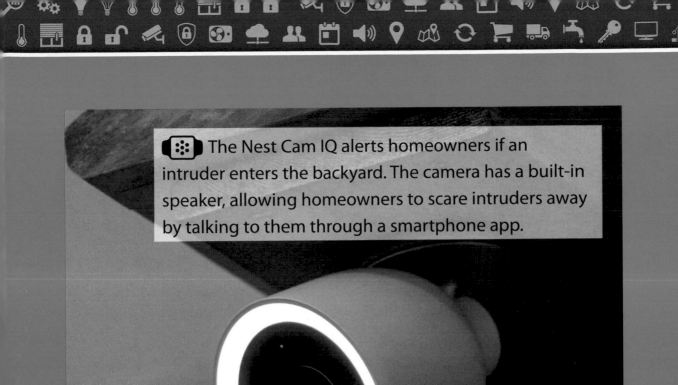

The Nest Cam IQ alerts homeowners if an intruder enters the backyard. The camera has a built-in speaker, allowing homeowners to scare intruders away by talking to them through a smartphone app.

Home security is a key area for smart development. Cameras and sensors will learn a person's usual routines. Then, if something unusual is happening, the sensors will detect it. This information then goes to a user's phone. And if the user subscribes to a service, the police can be alerted automatically.

Chapter 4

The city of Seattle's RainWatch system monitors rainfall in real-time with rain detectors that send data wirelessly. This allows the city to warn citizens when there is a chance of flooding.

Smart Cities

If people can build smart homes, why not build smart cities? Some cities are already trying. But what does it mean to be a smart city? As with houses, there are many ways that cities can be smart.

In many cities, drivers can access webcams of their commute on their smartphones. This helps them to see where there is traffic and plan an efficient route before leaving home.

In many cities, smart technology is booming in the area of **transportation**. Cities use technology to gather data about public transportation, driving, and parking. Then, users can find the most efficient ways to travel around the city.

Smart transportation programs work in real-time and are constantly updated. These programs do more than help people get where they are going more quickly. They also help the environment by cutting down on the use of **fossil fuels**.

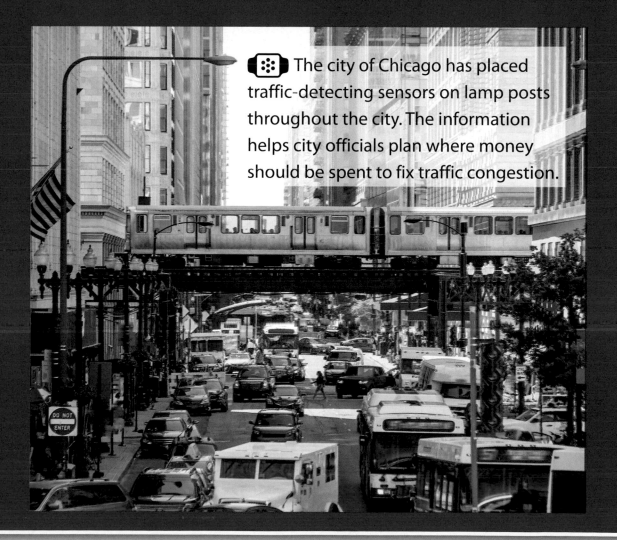

The city of Chicago has placed traffic-detecting sensors on lamp posts throughout the city. The information helps city officials plan where money should be spent to fix traffic congestion.

Some cities provide apps that help people connect with city services. For example, the city of Buenos Aires, Argentina, offers free **Wi-Fi** and city service apps. This means people can get city services, such as requesting a birth certificate, quickly and easily. This saves people time and effort.

Improving Happiness

Dubai is a city in the United Arab Emirates. Its residents can use a "Happiness Meter" when they visit most government service centers to rate their satisfaction with different aspects of the city. Users can choose from three options. They are, satisfied, neutral, or dissatisfied. City workers then see which areas of the city need the most improvement. They can use this data to provide better services.

Smart technology can also help with the design of cities themselves. Researchers use feedback from smart technology to identify problems, challenges, and solutions. For example, in Boston, Massachusetts, researchers are working on a way to let citizens plan bus routes. Community members can build models of bus routes using toy bricks and 3D projections. This leads to discussion and new ideas. Smart technology records the different models and proposals. Giving citizens an easier way to help improve their hometowns is the future of smart cities.

Officials in Louisville, Kentucky have given asthma sufferers inhalers with geographic sensors. This allows city officials to identify areas that have poor air quality based on usage of the inhaler.

Chapter 5

Cars produced by Tesla include an autopilot feature that enables the cars to drive and park themselves. However, as self-driving technology has not yet been perfected, drivers must be prepared to take the wheel at any time.

Smart Problems

Smart systems rely on technology. But technology sometimes fails, and these failures can have serious consequences. In 2016, a man was on the highway in his self-driving car. The car's sensors did not detect a truck, and the car crashed into it. The man in the self-driving car did not survive.

Another problem with smart technology is that **hackers** can attack networks. For example, smart TVs, internet-connected cameras, and baby monitors have all been hacked. This lets hackers see or hear what is going on inside the home. At the city level, hackers could do serious damage by attacking smart networks that control electricity or transportation.

Many home cameras get hacked because people have not changed their default passwords. Access to the camera lets thieves know what is available to steal and when owners leave home.

Hackers might also access the data that smart devices send to apps. That information also goes to the businesses that run the apps. Users have to think about how much information they are willing to share with businesses.

As with any technology, there are benefits and drawbacks. People will have to decide for themselves how smart they want their technology to be. To build a smart future, students can study science, technology, engineering, and math. These subjects will prepare students for exciting careers in smart technology.

In 2016, **Uber** was hacked, compromising the personal data of about **57 million** people.

About **36 percent** of people mistake **fake banking apps** for real ones, unknowingly giving hackers their login information.

1 What term do some people use when talking about smart technology?

2 What city allows residents to use a "Happiness Meter" to rate their satisfaction with the city?

3 What U.S. city lets community members build models of bus routes using toy bricks and 3D projections?

4 What smart assistant can place online orders, search the internet, and take notes?

5 What device gathers data for heart rate, respiration, body temperature, and air temperature?

6 What project allows the city of Seattle to monitor rainfall in real-time?

Answers

1. Internet of Things **2.** Dubai **3.** Boston **4.** Amazon's Alexa **5.** A fitness tracker **6.** RainWatch

Key Words

app: a computer program that completes a task

data: information represented by facts and numbers

fossil fuels: energy sources, such as coal and oil, that come from plants and animals that have been dead for millions of years

hackers: people who illegally access computers

interactive: able to respond to a user's actions or commands

networks: systems of computers and devices that are connected to one another

smartphones: mobile phones that do many of the same functions as computers

thermostat: a device that controls temperature

transportation: a system of moving people and goods from one place to another

Wi-Fi: allows devices to wirelessly connect to the internet and to each other

Index

Log on to www.av2books.com

AV² by Weigl brings you media enhanced books that support active learning. Go to www.av2books.com, and enter the special code found on page 2 of this book. You will gain access to enriched and enhanced content that supplements and complements this book. Content includes video, audio, weblinks, quizzes, a slide show, and activities.

AV² Online Navigation

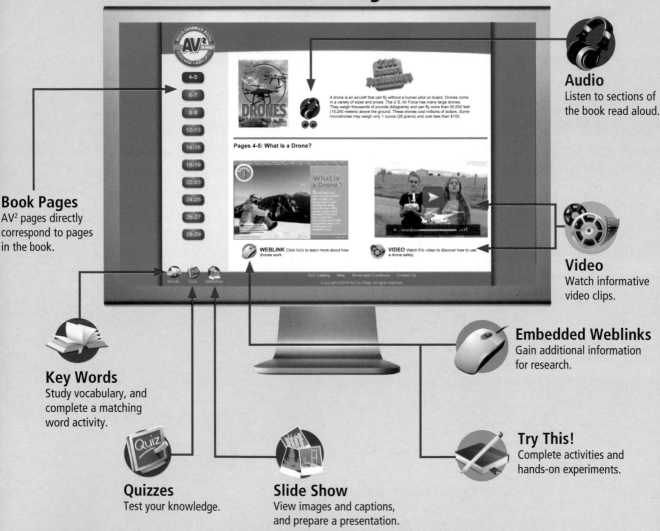

Audio
Listen to sections of the book read aloud.

Book Pages
AV² pages directly correspond to pages in the book.

Video
Watch informative video clips.

Key Words
Study vocabulary, and complete a matching word activity.

Embedded Weblinks
Gain additional information for research.

Try This!
Complete activities and hands-on experiments.

Quizzes
Test your knowledge.

Slide Show
View images and captions, and prepare a presentation.

AV² was built to bridge the gap between print and digital. We encourage you to tell us what you like and what you want to see in the future.

Sign up to be an AV² Ambassador at www.av2books.com/ambassador.

Due to the dynamic nature of the Internet, some of the URLs and activities provided as part of AV² by Weigl may have changed or ceased to exist. AV² by Weigl accepts no responsibility for any such changes. All media enhanced books are regularly monitored to update addresses and sites in a timely manner. Contact AV² by Weigl at 1-866-649-3445 or av2books@weigl.com with any questions, comments, or feedback.